Disaster Management Techniques

Water Harvesting and Storage

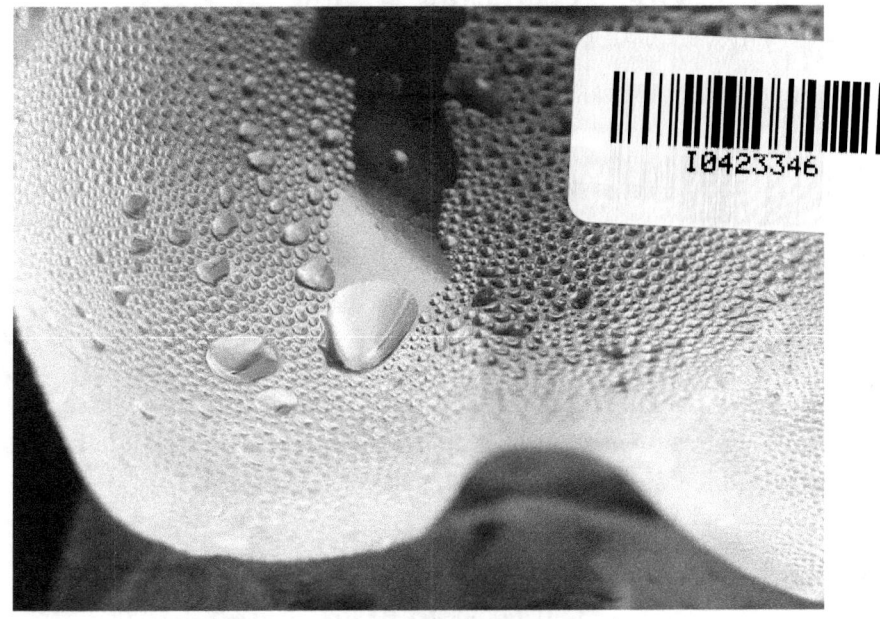

I0423346

Dueep Jyot Singh

Survival Series

Mendon Cottage Books

JD-Biz Publishing

Download Free Books!

http://MendonCottageBooks.com

Our books are available at

1. Amazon.com

2. Barnes and Noble

3. Itunes

4. Kobo

5. Smashwords

6. Google Play Books

Download Free Books!

http://MendonCottageBooks.com

Table of Contents

Introduction

However much we like reading adventure stories, where the hero is lost in the desert, and he knows that he has to use his own creativity or the imagination of the writer in order to survive, many of us cannot think of a scenario when we may find ourselves in a situation where we need to find water.

Nevertheless, this book is going to tell you all about the ways and means in which you can find water, which is of course the most important resource for survival, now that the 21st-century has reached the stage of natural disasters every year, thanks to climatic changes, and human beings fiddling with the natural ecological makeup of Mother Nature.

Either keep this book with you, when you go out hiking in the desert or in the woods, or just put it on your e-book reader to be browsed through, when your city has been subjected to Typhoon Tanya or hurricane Harriet or Earthquake Edwina and you are caught outside in an alien atmosphere.

One hopes that one does not find oneself in that condition, but being an ostrich in the 21st century is the easiest way to be called a "typical helpless excuse for a human being who cannot and will not accept reality but prefers living in a 'that cannot happen to me' dream world."

Unfortunately, there are a number of us out there, who belong to this category. An earthquake is always going to happen somewhere in Japan. A hurricane is always going to happen in coastal regions, far away from you. A typhoon, what is that, no question of it happening in your area, because nobody heard of that word ever in your city.

Well, this book is an eye-opener for all these ostriches. Natural calamities are going to occur every year, however much scientists and politicians and naysayers say that they have these situations under control! Behold me blinking.

Since when has man been able to control the fury of nature? He may be so scientifically advanced that he can predict earthquakes, like the Chinese and the Japanese did more than 3,000 years ago, and can have an advanced warning on hurricanes and thus evacuate the people in that area as soon as possible. But no human being has had the power of Canute standing on the seashore, and ordering the waves to stop, because he is the king, and nature has to obey his orders! However much escapist novelists talk about wizards and powerful magicians, capable of controlling the forces of nature, never has been done, never can be done by an ordinary helpless human being.

As a scientist, and capable of telling you the truth, let me give you the real life scenario, which you are going to be facing in the future. Thanks to the experiments done underground in the 20th century, including underwater and underground nuclear tests, by a number of my one track minded scientist brethren, the physical makeup of the earth's internal structure and tectonic plates has changed irreversibly.

You know it. I know it. But we would rather have some half sleepy scientist say that that is not true. And we believe it, because we would rather have someone tell us that the wolf is not at our door, and never can be because he says so, while we are trying our best to survive a wolf attack on our family!

Consider that to be the exact state of how nature is going to work, all over the World. From now on in the 21st-century, you are going to undergo water deprivation, food deprivation, catastrophe, natural upheavals, and the situation is going to worsen, however much you called me a Cassandra and wish that I could be burnt at the stake for being a witch speaking evil.

So here are some time-tested tips for survival used by mankind down the ages, depending on which part of the World you find yourself, and what the available natural resources there are.

Going exploring is fun, as long as you know that you have access to shelter, food, and water.

Many people are under the impression that if you find yourself in the desert area, you are definitely not going to have any sources of water available to you there. That is because we have auto suggested ourselves into thinking that desert means complete dryness. However, many of us do not know that there are periods in the desert where it rains, and for a while, the desert is completely green, taking for example, the Sahara or the Kalahari Desert. Unfortunately, because it does not have lots of trees growing there, so that the water could at least be retained in that particular green microclimate and tree induced ecosystem, this water sinks back into the earth and goes underground again. And so we have the dry surface upon which the sun shines unrelentingly.

Did you know that a number of the desert areas, all over the World were once green and fertile lands, where civilizations flourished in ancient times, and where you had plenty of water and greenery? With natural climatic changes, the water level on the surface and underground began to dry up, and only those plants which could survive in that very harsh climate flourished there.

Man was the first to leave that area because he cannot do without water. However, even in a desert, you are going to find some places even now, where you can get water with a little bit of exploration and digging. I was reading Peter O'Donnell's book written under the pseudonym of Madeleine Brent [as a sly salute to his greatest creation Modesty Blaise] – The Golden Urchin.

This is the story of a young white girl brought up among the Australian aborigines, and she knows everything about survival. One day, while exploring the desert of the Australian outback, she sees a young white man dying of malnutrition, dehydration, and starvation. According to her, that white man is so foolish because food and water is right under his very nose, but he does not know how to gain access to it. Nor can he smell it out!

Naturally, she saved him by collecting water and getting a number of proteinaceous edible grubs together, and even though he protested that he was not going to eat insects, she overruled him by feeding them to him. And then when he got back some of his energy, she kept trying to teach him how to recognize the sources of water by following the flight of insects, or looking for places where water could have been collected in crevices or near rocks.

We civilized human beings cannot smell out water, even though as a child I knew when it was going to rain because I could feel the rain smell in my nostrils, and then 99.9 % of the time I was right, because we were living in the mountains and in the forests!

But as I grew up, I began to live in the heavily polluted air of water deprived cities and lost this particular faculty, even though sometimes, even now I can sniff the air and say, "Well, it is going to rain soon," and the people all around me say, "Oh golly, is that hundred percent crank predicting rain again?" Especially in the desert. And then when it rains within the next eight hours, they ask me how did I know that it was going to rain?

And I have to look suitably mysterious, because one cannot explain such things and instincts. Anyway, talking about water, remember that human beings can do without food at a pinch, and even do without shelter, but they need water.

What is going to happen to you if you do not have water around? For the first 24 hours, you are going to manage especially if you have some shelter and food. After sometime, you are going to find yourself getting dehydrated.

If you do not have a shelter or any food, this weakening is going to happen faster. Your mental strength as well as your physical strength is going to be depleted really quickly.

Food, water, and shelter for yourself is your first priority. When you find yourself in the open in inclement weather, protect yourself from the wind and the rain.

Three days without any water and your body system is going to go into emergency mode in order to preserve all the liquids which are already present in it.

I was reading Dick Francis's amazing Book, *Smokescreen*, where the hero is locked away in a car with his hands handcuffed to the steering wheel. All this action takes place in an African animal reserve in South Africa. The physical and mental torment of a man who does not have any food, nor any water has been described amazingly well. But when a professional who is adept in the art of survival reads this book, he is going to talk about a couple of points, Mr. Francis overlooked.[1]

The hero Edward Lincoln had a huge man sized handkerchief in his pocket. He could have placed it over his face in order to protect it from the sun pouring down through the car window screen, thus preventing sunburn.

At night, he could have placed the handkerchief, outside the window, hanging out, – and with the window shut, thus making sure that it did not fall out of the car and out of reach – so that by the morning, that large handkerchief could be drenched with the dew collected on the glass of the window, and thus permeating the handkerchief.

The handkerchief would not have gotten completely wet, because dew does not work that way, except if the atmosphere is really muggy and full of humidity, but at least it would not be just an ordinary piece of cloth coming to no use at all during an emergency situation.

---

[1] I am not going to talk about one particular aspect of survival – getting rid of body fluids like urine. Professional disaster management experts are not going to let this fluid go to waste, especially when there is absolutely no source of water anywhere.

Naturally, we shudder at the thought of using this water in a purified form for drinking, but when experts talk man-to-man among their masculine trainees, they are going to talk about this particular survival technique. This of course is a last ditch extreme solution, and you are definitely not going to resort to it, because of the high salt content which is going to lead to ultimate kidney failure, within two – three days. It is almost as bad as drinking blood and/or saltwater, in order to survive.

So remember that natural dew collected on the leaves, or any other surface which is flat, is capable of giving you anywhere between 3 tablespoons full of water to more, depending on how flat that surface is.

Using a Survival Blanket

Let me tell you all about one marvelous lightweight survival item I have in my adventuring kit, especially when I am camping out in the forests. It is a comparatively new innovation called a survival blanket. It was first made for astronauts, but nowadays, it is getting to be very common among people, who enjoy outdoor activities and find themselves trapped in all sorts of weather conditions.

http://www.ebay.com/itm/Outdoor-Sports-Adventure-Emergency-Tent-Blanket-Survival-Accident-prevention-/351748522611

This is how it looks, and I got a pack of 3 for about $0.75, and I have been using it not as a disposable blanket to regulate my body temperature in harsh weather conditions, but as the best surface for the collection of dew, outside my tent.

But then you have to get up at dawn, before sunrise in order to collect all that water, otherwise it is going to disappear with the first rays of the sun!

According to the seller, this is for one-time use. Bah, say I, because I have used one of these sheets, about eight or nine times for different activities, and then packed it up again for future use. It does not tear so easily. I also used this as a second sheet, and as a roof shelter over some twigs. They work really well.

Whatever the sellers may say, this is definitely not a substitute for a warm blanket or any other source of natural warmth. It is just a flat covering and lightweight. So do not take a pack of these, when you go out hiking and forget about the necessary hiking clothing that is going to help you survive inclement weather.

The good thing about water is that it is going to be available in some form or the other in all climates and environments upon the earth. I remember hiking on the mountains, with a friend, who spent her time groaning and moaning and saying that this trek was not something she was used to, and I was really cruel to her, taking her to see the snows on the mountains.

Naturally, she never accompanied me again., kill joys I can do without. Anyway, we reached the snow peaks, and she had another thing to complain about. Her water bottle was empty. Where would she get water? She would die of cold right there. Oh, I was so stupid, not to tell her to put more bottles of mineral water in her pack, until I had to shake her.

And then I said, "Snow – water – duh!" And she finally got the idea. Snow was water! Believe it or not, there are some hothouse flowers out there, whose brains do not work outside their normal environment which is living in cities, and not moving an inch out of that particular environment!

And that is why when they find themselves stranded in the snow, they are going to just sit down and moan that their cell phones are not working in those high altitudes and they cannot call for help! These people are not going to move a finger in order to help themselves and if you find them along with you, you will either have to take very steady measures to make sure that they are not drags and hindrances in your bid for survival, or just tell them at point-blank range – "We are pushing on to a place where we can get shelter and food, you can sit here and freeze."

See how they change their minds and scramble after you, incipient hysterics forgotten.

This book is going to give you plenty of information on how you can find different sources of water, in different situations like in temperate zones, tropical zones, deserts, and even mountains.

When I was a child, living in the mountains, and we were hundred percent sure that the water sources would be adulterated because of little pieces of twigs, bark, and leaves, falling into the base's water filtration tanks, it was a given that we never drank water directly from the tap.

My grandmother always placed a thin cloth of Muslin over an earthenware clay pot in order to filter the water. And then we drank that filtered water. In the rainy season, we boiled the water, before it was cooled down and then placed into different water containers.

So that is how we learned instinctively to filter the water, before we drank it, especially when we were out exploring in the jungles. And there were so many water sources over there, like waterfalls, lakes, streams, natural rivulets, and even rain water collected in large leaves.

We had a container into which we would place all that precious water after filtering it with a large handkerchief borrowed off dad. And thus we did not swallow lots of weeds, leaves, poly wiggles, water bugs, and other things in the water.

But you say, you are in a situation where there is absolutely no way in which you can purify the water. You do not have water purification tablets with you. Well, think very carefully. Would you like to drink water from an adulterated source found naturally and full of dirt, bugs, bacteria, and other harmful critters?

But before I teach you the ways and methods in which you are going to filter water before it is ready for you to drink, you have to find out how you can find water in the wilderness.

Finding Water in the Wilderness

This is for when you are in a tropical or a temperate region. It is also going to work well in other environments and climates.

Your first priority is to look for general sources of water, the natural sources of lakes, streams, rivulets, and rivers. If the water is clear and flowing free, you are lucky, because that means that the bacteria have not had time to sit still and proliferate in stagnant water.

This water is normally going to be found in small rivulets and streams. Rivers are a total hazard, nowadays, because half of the rivers which were blue and clear, during my childhood are brown, muddy, poisonous, and polluted today. However, if there is a rivulet full of clear water, rushing down the mountain, you are lucky, because that has been made up of melted snow and has not had any chance of getting polluted by man-made chemical wastes.

When we went exploring in the forests as children, we were told never to drink from ponds and lakes, because the water was stagnant in them. It never got a chance to move. That is why it was full of fungi, bacteria and other not so healthy and noxious things which could make you really sick.

Using Your Natural Senses to Find Water

Oh, the sweet sound of a water fall in the woods.

Ears

So how did we get to know where the water was? This is where we used our five senses. We stood perfectly still and let our ears do the searching for us.

Running water has a clear and distinct sound and you can hear it clearly, even if you are far away from it.

As children, our target was the local waterfall, about 5 km into the forest. We did not have compasses, but we used our ears to orient ourselves in the general direction of the waterfall and managed to reach it, 99 times out of 100. The only time we did not reach the waterfall was when it began to rain and we had to take shelter in one of the caves.

Using Your Eyes

Well, if by chance you stood there for about half an hour and cannot hear any source of running water, you are now going to use your eyes.

Look out for insect swarms. In reality, you are going to find them really annoying, especially when they are made up of midges, flies, and also bees. In the wilderness, these swarms are what are going to save you. They are going to take you directly to the nearest source of water. Also look very carefully on the ground.

You are going to see a number of little animal tracks leading you to places where those animals found water to drink. And if it is early morning or evening, look at the sky and look at the flight of the birds in the forest they know where the water is.

Animal tracks are best seen in the desert because you can find them clearly. In the forest areas, you are going to look at the insects on the ground, and the direction in which they are going. In the desert, flocks of birds are going to take you to the nearest water source.

Using Your Nose

Now you are going to follow your nose. Unfortunately, man has forgotten his natural instinct of sniffing out a water source, down the ages, but this following of the nose is looking at your location and environment. Water always flows downwards or downhill. So if you find a valley or a gully, there is a chance that once upon a time, some water flowed down it. Just begin going towards lower ground from higher ground, and you are going to find some water source somewhere.

While you are walking, be on the lookout for holes within or around rocks. If there is even the littlest bit of greenery between them, like grasses and ferns, that is where the water is. If the surface of any rock is covered with moss, that is good, because that means that there is enough of water seeping from somewhere, to make a mossy carpet.

You are going to peel off the layer of moss from the stone or the surface and touch the under portion. If it is wet, that means you are near a source of water, which may be rainwater or natural water. Green moss in itself is a sign for a source of water.

Collecting Rainwater

One can only pack so much bottled mineral water

If you are in an open area, where it is raining and raining often, you are lucky because you have a perpetual source of hydration, and clean water. Do not collect the first showers of rainwater to drink, in an urban area. It is definitely not safe to drink it because this water brings with it dirt and dust particles, and polluted chemicals.

However, with the passage of time, and with a number of showers taking place during the season, the atmosphere gets cleared of the side effects of civilization, and you can use that rainwater collected in containers in your house for a number of purposes. Like washing and drinking only after filtering and boiling.

But here we are in the jungle. We do not have a container. We are going to make containers out of large leaves.

Conical Container

This is how we did it, when we were children. We collected the largest leaves we could find. And then we used to take tiny little pieces of sticks and pin the edges together. Soon we would have a huge flat "plate" about 18 inches in width, circular in shape, and ready to be turned into any sort of container.

Then we use to put our little fists into the middle of the leaf "plate" and slowly begin turning the plate into a conical dunce cap. Visualize Merlin's hat, when you are making the cone.

One portion of this cone is going to be completely broad and open, looking just like the paper container in which you put fish and chips. Right at the bottom is that small gap, which you are going to turn over and pin with some more little pieces of sticks, so that nothing you put into that container flows out.

Pin the edges of the cone, to make a conical container.

Incidentally, I found this excellent URL, where you can see how to make natural leaf containers by methods they use traditionally in Nepal. And the moment I read Saal leaves, back I was to my childhood, making these containers with banana leaves and Saal leaves, but not in Nepal but in the forests of Saranda, as well as the banana laden forests of South India.

http://tasteofnepal.blogspot.in/2012/03/leaf-plates-of-nepal-tapari-duna-bota.html

What fun we had. The plates were called "Pattal." The containers were called "donnas." Even today, in many parts of the East, if you go to a religious place or take part in a religious ceremony, you are going to be fed on one of these containers.

In ancient times, in many parts of the East, a prospective son-in-law was asked by the bride's family to make a banana leaf plate and a container and the quicker he made it, and how dexterously he made it was the measure in how eligible he was to marry into the family! The plate of course had to be leakproof and so had to be the bowls, into which he would ladle liquid curries and soups to feed his future in-laws!

https://www.youtube.com/watch?v=zkEmWxv6N7A

Here is a URL uploaded by a lady, in a tropical region, where there are plenty of banana leaves. You may want to practice the making of these cups, at home.

Naturally, when you are in a jungle you are not going to have a stapler with you. So you are going to be using sharp little pieces of twigs and wood and slivers of bamboo if you can get them, in order to pin the pieces together.

Along with these natural containers, you are going to use any other hollow containers to collect rainwater.

Now let me show you how you are going to be collecting Rainwater, with the help of large sheets, tarpaulins, or any flat surface.

You are going to tie the four corners of these sheets and tarpaulins, around the trunks of trees, at about chest level. Put a small piece of rock in the middle of the tarpaulin so that you can get a depression. And then allow the water to collect there.

If you have a larger container, you can combine both methods of water harvesting by tying the tarpaulin in such a way that all the water goes straight into your container or pot, making sure that it is not wasted or it does not overflow.

You may want to try out this water harvesting process in your yard, if it has been raining for a number of days. Then you can be sure that the water that you are going to get is really pure. Also, you have a number of containers ready at hand, and they are going to collect all the water for you.

When we lived in high-altitude areas, where it rained 300 days out of 365, and the rest of the time, it was either moist, muggy, sleeting or drizzling, my grandmother was always in a state of early morning exasperation.

That was because, when she woke up at dawn in order to make tea for the rest of the adults in the family, – some duties were the prerogative of the oldest lady, in the family, the matriarch, and they are being followed, even today, these ladies do the cooking for the whole family, in many parts of the East – she always had to go out into the garden.

That was because her exasperating little cubs had picked up all the utensils in the kitchen and put them in the garden, the previous night in order to collect rainwater which fell during the night!

So we learned water harvesting as babies! We loved that rainwater, to drink, – straight from the utensils, and pouring the rest over ourselves, if we were not dancing in the rain, we *were* little savages –because we felt that it was pure. Besides that, father used to use this rainwater in his car batteries instead of distilled water. So we knew it was one hundred percent safe!

Collecting the Early Morning Dew

This was a method shown to me by a Commando uncle, who told me that he could get one liter of water just by taking a walk in the early morning through tall grass.

This was after he had tied up some clothes, which were capable of absorbing water – natural fiber clothes, like cotton – or if that was not available, he would tie up tufts of fine grass and then go walking and stomping in any green area where the grass grew, for about an hour. The moment the clothes were saturated, the water was wrung out into the water container tied to his belt and the process repeated again.

But look out for early-morning insects, snakes, and also make sure that the grass or the plants through which you are stomping are not poisonous. As children, we used to go walking in the dew on our lawn at dawn, bare feet, because according to ancient knowledge, this massaging of the pressure points on our feet's soles would strengthen our eyes and our systems I still remember how wet our pajama ankles used to get.

Also, dancing in the dew, when the rest of the World is still half asleep, in the early morning is a practice which only little pagans can appreciate, especially in the mountains or in a jungle! Funny, we never bothered about insects, especially when we ran through tall grasses day in day out, 24/7!

Getting Water from Vegetation and Fruit

Did you know that cactuses, vegetables, fruit, and any plants with pulps and also their roots have a large percentage of liquid water? If you have any of these plants at hand, all you have to do is collect them, and mash them into a mass, which is going to be full of pulpy tissue and liquid. It does not take the place of solid honest-to-goodness H_2O, but it serves as something which is going to prevent you from being dehydrated.

I was watching that really cute movie, The Gods Must Be Crazy, about the wish man in the Kalahari Desert. This is an area where there are absolutely no rocks and water is of course at a premium. So the people there know how to harvest water by putting out leaves at night so that the morning dew can collect there ready to be drunk at dawn.

Along with that, they know how to grate the roots, until they have a pulp, and then as the narrator says, just take a handful, and squeeze to get water to drink. Remember never ever to grate the roots of the cassava, especially if you are in Africa. It is deadly poisonous.

You may want to go through this list.

https://en.wikipedia.org/wiki/List_of_poisonous_plants

However, if you are in a tropical region, and you have plenty of fruit around, you are lucky. Because that means you have an automatic source of fruit sugar, fruit pulp, nourishing food, as well as water.

Look for the nearest source of coconuts. Drink only the water of green and unripe coconuts and never those which are ripe. That is because ripe coconut water is laxative in nature and that means you are going to get even more dehydrated.

Of course you can chew on the coconut meat of ripe coconuts in order to get plenty of nourishment. Of course you are not going to let that water go to waste, are you? Put it in a container and wet your whole body, especially the exposed parts with that coconut water. This is the best natural moisturizer which is going to prevent your skin from drying up.

Water from Plant Transpiration

This is a natural water harvesting method, which you can use, especially if you are in an area with lots of green leafy trees and you recognize them as not being poisonous. A part of this procedure is described in Dick Francis's Smokescreen referred to above. The hero imprisoned in the car has a plastic bag in his pocket.

You can read the excerpt here –

http://tinyurl.com/ztfv35u

Let us assume that you do have a plastic bag, which is large and which you are going to use for collecting water, especially through the scientific process of transpiration. During transpiration, the water from the roots is circulated up to the leafy stomata on the underside of the leaves, and during transpiration in the sunlight, this water gets evaporated and escapes to the atmosphere.

We are going to be trapping that escaping water.

This is going to be done early in the morning so that the transpired water throughout the day can collect in whatever container that you have turned into a bag. The larger it is, the better it is for you. You may want to put something weighty like a rock inside the bag so that it weighs down. This is where the water is going to collect. Now, tie up this bag around a really leafy green branch with lots and lots of leaves. All the transpired water which would have escaped in the atmosphere during the day is now collecting in the bag.

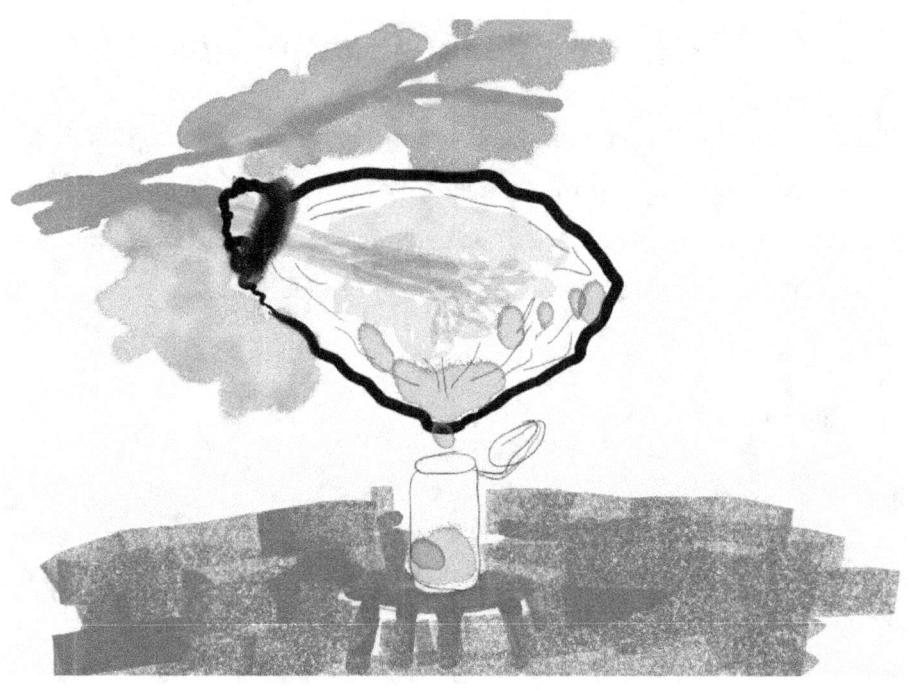

This can only be done by a person who knows that the trees around him are not poisonous. I gave you a URL above, telling you about a number of poisonous plants, and these include cedar and pine.

Naturally, the larger the container is, the more water you can collect, also from the outside of the sheeting, dripping down into the container from the weighed down conical portion, externally. This is the moisture in the atmosphere, especially if the weather is muggy and you leave it overnight outside. Water is also collecting inside through transpiration, and it is going to be stored in the container when you think that you have a good amount of water at hand.

Getting Water from Rock Crevices and Hollows in Trees

Remember that the sources of water which you get from transpiration, rock crevices, and tree hollows are limited in quantity, but they are much better than absolutely not a drop of water to drink. If you are lost in the desert and dreaming of water, even a little bit of murky water is going to be a godsend, even if it makes you sick.

I was watching Dirk Bogarde's comeuppance at the hands of Willie Garvin in *Modesty Blaise* and he has been staked out in the hot sun as punishment for being such a nasty villain. He is totally dehydrated and thirsty. And he is asking for liquid sustenance, of the only liquid which he drinks, of anybody who is around and willing to listen, "champagne… champagne."

We are not going to get any champagne, under no circumstances in the desert. We are going to be collecting little bits of water where this precious store has collected over the passage of time.

If you find some bird droppings around any rock crevice, it means that there is some water somewhere. It is going to be between rocks, or collected in a crack.

You are going to take a stick, wrap up a piece of cloth around it, and poke it in that particular crevice and crack. If you are lucky, it is going to come out wet. You cannot see the source of water, because you are too large and could not crawl between a very narrow crack or two pieces of stone.

If the birds and the insects are drinking it, you can manage to drink it, even though you may find yourself coming down with stomach flu. That is, if the water is contaminated. Water in itself does not go bad. It is only when the water has been contaminated by external sources, that is when the danger starts.

If you have tapped a deep water source behind the rocks, you may want to try some digging in the sand. The water which has collected behind the rocks is going to seep through the sand and fill up the hole, to which you have an easier access.

Digging a Sill

This is normally called an underground sill and if you have the energy to dig a hole in the sand, this is going to serve you better because it is going to collect a substantial amount of water, especially when you know that the water is there and you know how much you are going to get over a given period of time.

This is normally done in areas where you can see some greenery, also, where the ground is damp. Start digging, and the water underground is going to start seeping into the hole. Digging can also be done under a cliff, in a dry bed of a river, in low areas, in valleys, and also if you see a desert lake which has gone dry and recognize the first dune of sand. That means there is water in that desert, or in those hills.

The water is not going to be clean because it has come out of the sand. You will need to filter it with a cloth.

Along with this, you can also make a number of holes, if you have many containers and plastic sheeting available.

Firstly, you are going to use your energy and dig a hole with any digging tool available. In ancient times, when people did not know about metal to be used, to make a digging implement, they used anything sharp and strong enough in order to dig and well, they used their hands. If you have a sharp metal implement, so much the better for you.

This hole is going to be made in any area which has lots of sunlight throughout the day. That is because we are going to be using the process of condensation. If you have a hollow tube so much the better, because that means that you can run the tubing out of the container placed in the hole, and drink water straight from the water source without removing the plastic sheet.

It is going to take a little while to dig the hole, which should be 3 feet wide and 2 feet deep. Why so deep, you may say? It is because at this particular depth, you are going to get lots of moisture. Condensation is going to occur, when this moisture tries to escape out of the hole and gets blocked by the plastic sheet covering the mouth of the hole completely. You are going to dig another smaller hole into that pit, into which you are going to place the container.

Remember to weigh down the plastic sheet with a rock so that there is a weighed down depression like a sharply inverted cone, right above your container. That means there is not going to be any wastage of water. Place the tubing in the container, and after you have placed the container in the hole, check that the tubing runs out of that pit properly, and is easily accessible to you.

Remember that you are going to get just one liter of water per day, because the condensation progress and process is really slow. That is why you may need a lot of pits, plastic sheets, and other water sources, apart from the source to get a good steady supply of water. This naturally is going to be made in any place where you see a little bit of green foliage. That means the microclimate is already present and all you need is to collect the moisture.

This transpiration process, along with condensation is going to give you pure water.

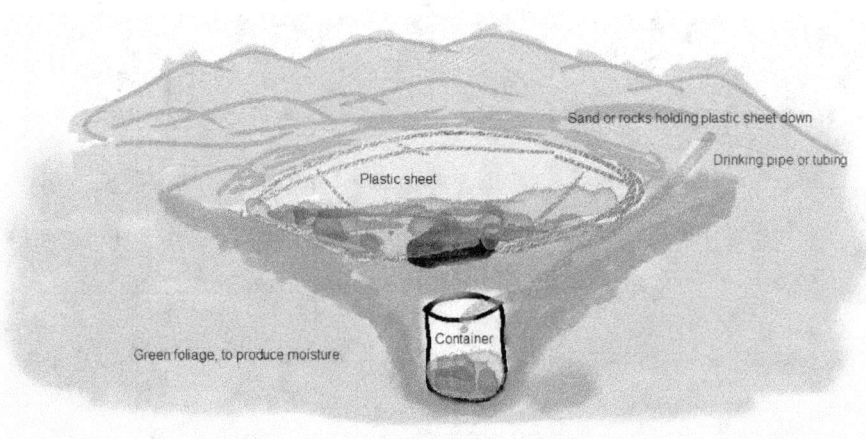

I would suggest using all your survival blankets because after all they are large, flat surfaces and able to capture all the condensation. The best quality ones are the Space All Weather Blankets because they do not tear as easily.

Water Filtering

Under such circumstances, any source of natural water especially drinking water is going to be contaminated. That is why you have to look for filtered potable water.

Here, we are using some natural products, like sand, gravel, and wood charcoal, considering that we have got the charcoal from our campfire in the desert or outdoors. We are definitely not going to be using the charcoal which is dug out from the ground, because that is a different type of charcoal altogether.

Just for general information we have written a number of disaster management/survival books, in different atmospheres, in this particular series. You may want to look at them also.

A Beginner's Guide to Campfires - http://tinyurl.com/jjvko8a

Beginner's Guide to Forest Survival - http://tinyurl.com/jyyrhke

Survival Skills You Cannot Live Without - http://tinyurl.com/hlr3fvh

Now here we are, with some natural filtering products ready at hand. Surprisingly enough, charcoal has been used for filtering water, for ages, because I remember my grandmother talking about how charcoal filters were a part and parcel of every household in the rainy season. This was a traditional way with which water was purified. Sand was not available there in very large quantities in that particular area. So they had to make do with charcoal, and gravel.

So here is the traditional way in which water has been filtered for millenniums, and we as children enjoyed doing this experiment in our science projects at school, being thrilled with the water coming out so clean in the containers.

This experiment was shown to us by our science teacher, who used a clay pot, with a hole at the bottom, under which he put a glass container so that we could see the water flowing into the container.

He covered the hole at the bottom with a muslin cloth because according to him; we did not want our fresh water source being contaminated with pieces of sand and gravel, did we?

After that, he put a layer of charcoal over the cloth, and because we had plenty of charcoal available from kitchen fires, which still was the source of cooking in many parts of the country at that time, we had a really thick layer of charcoal. Remember that ash does not work here. You have to break up the charcoal into small pieces, so that you have plenty of carbon content to filter the water through.

Over that, he placed a thick layer of sand. One third of the clay pot was charcoal, and one third was sand. The last and uppermost layer was gravel which filtered out the large particles of sediment.

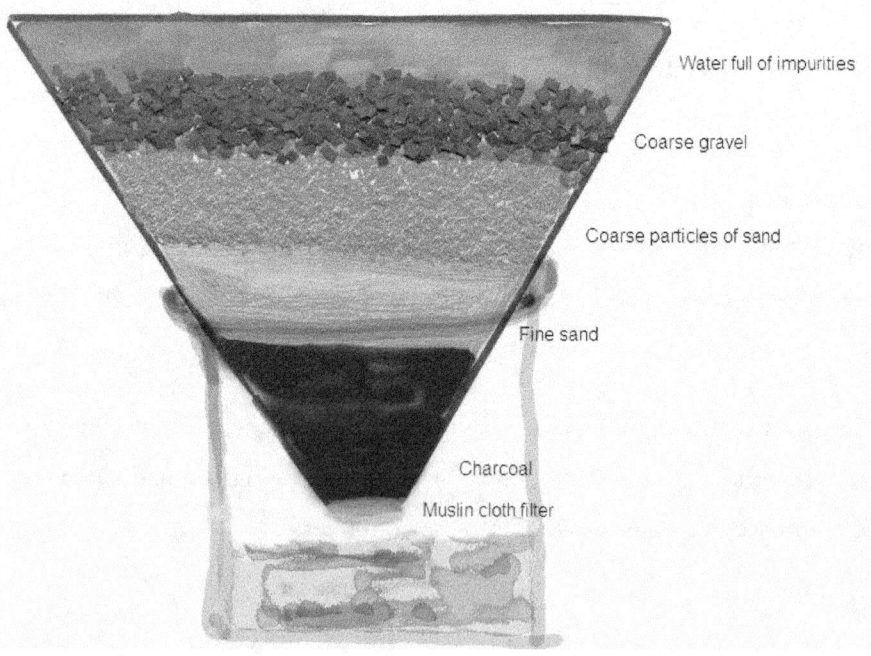

Water full of impurities

Coarse gravel

Coarse particles of sand

Fine sand

Charcoal

Muslin cloth filter

He told us that if we wanted the water to be really pure, we would do as our ancestors did and place twigs of plants like sacred basil, neem, and other healthy herbs, between the layers so that their good qualities also went into the water!

And then he poured really dirty water upon the gravel, making sure that the layers were not disturbed. After that the pot was placed on top of the glass container, and he told us "alright kids, it is time for you to go home, you can see how much of water has been filtered by tomorrow, and this is your home – project for the week, 20 marks for the most innovative filter."

One point, when you are choosing the course gravel. Make sure that it is made up of stones or pebbles, and is definitely not mud!

The charcoal and all the layers get rid of all the sediments. You may not find really crystal-clear water, which can be bottled and sold to credulous buyers, but you are going to get clean and potable water.

Anyway, we had plenty of fun making these filters, especially when we already had traditional drums and containers and ancient filters somewhere in the cellars and just needed to go and ask the town elders whether we were doing the filtering process right!

Many of them told us that their more enterprising and innovative grandfathers attached a small tap/pipe to the bottom of the containers and drums, so that they could keep tapping water or get a continuous flow, 24/7, instead of having all of the water collecting in a container underneath the filter.

By the way, I asked my father whether he had ever made this filter, once he grew up and had left his village, and he said of course. This was how he filtered water in areas, where one could not quite trust the water filtration plants, and if there was a chance of any sort of infection, he boiled the result, before he drank it.

Boiling Water Tip!

And then I asked him, what if he was in a place where he did not have a utensil in which to boil the water, but he had access to a heating source like a gas flame, he asked me to do this really interesting experiment.

For this, you need a really thick paper bag. You are now going to fill it up with the water. Place it on the source of heat, and wait for the paper bag to catch fire. Be very surprised, when it does not catch fire.

That is because the water prevents the fire from setting the paper bag alight. And there you are you have instant hot water.

He told me he had learned this trick in America, in the 60s, where an American friend had told him that if he had access to a gas flame or, as was common in those times, a gas jet, he would just fill some water from the sink, and heat it!

The friend used this water for shaving early in the morning and had a large supply of easily accessible really thick paper bags, always present in his suitcase!

Here is a very interesting URL, about how you can make a water filter at home, just for practice!

http://www.wikihow.com/Make-a-Water-Filter

So try these experiments in filtering, and you are going to be surprised at the taste of the water, which may possibly not taste so chlorinated, or so chemically ridden, after it has gone through sand and charcoal.

Out There in the Cold

Just because it is cold outside, it does not mean that you should neglect proper and adequate sources of water.

You are going to ask me if ever I found myself out there, trapped in the cold, outdoors, with no shelter or source of heat or even adequate clothing. Well, I can tell you that it was only once in a lifetime that I found myself trapped on a high mountain pass – way back in 1986 – on the way to Ladakh, on the Zojhi- La Pass, 5,000 feet above sea level.

Luckily, it was July, even though we were surrounded by snow clad peaks. The weather was not very cold, or it is possible that we youngsters did not quite feel the cold, clad as we were in sweaters, caps, overcoats, corduroy trousers, and hiking boots.

Anyway, our army convoy had broken down at about 8:30 at night, and there we were out in the open. We were not worried about shelter, because we had our sleeping bags and we had the road on which to sleep [!] or inside the trucks.

The soldiers immediately taking it for granted that this was part and parcel of their daily life's adventure theme immediately lifted up their driver's seats, showing us enclosed hollows, where lots of things were stored.

From there, they took out Primus stoves, chicken in packets, spices, homemade bread, either made by their wives and packaged in airtight packages or flour, with which they would knead dough in order to make fresh bread.

I really cannot forget the wonderful aroma of food cooking at that high-altitude, and nor can I forget that unforgettable delicious meal we had there. While it was being cooked on different stoves, I and my younger brother were going up and down the convoy line, doing our version of inspections of what was cooking!

One stove was used specifically for melting snow. For this, water from a canteen was put to the boil, because snow from the mountains when melted, on its own tastes really awful. We learned to recognize snow and ice that was old, and had come down the mountains, in a thaw or through the rain.

This was crystalline in nature and it was easy to collect it by just hitting it with a heavy pocketknife. I think we used a metal tire rim in order to collect lots of snow to bring to the water melting kettle.

It was then added slowly to the boiling water. Snow added directly to the hot kettle would only get scorched.

Also, we were told that only dimwitted tenderfeet ate snow directly, in order to quench their raging, burning, and high-altitude thirst. This was the easiest way in which you could get really sick, because your body's normal temperature would go down. Any sort of speeding up of your metabolism at a high-altitude area was definitely not desirable, and this would happen because your body would try to equalize the temperature.

And how could that be done when you were shoveling snow into yourself? So we had plenty of nicely boiled and then filtered snow water, lots and lots of it, and all our canteens were filled with this water for future glug glugs, throughout the next day.

Incidentally, as I was so curious to know what I could do with the snow and get drinking water from it, if I did not have access to a source of heat, here was the tip given to me.

Put the snow in small quantities, to your already present source of water and shake it along, until it has melted. Keep doing that regularly and replenishing the water in your canteen with handfuls of freshwater snow and you are never going to be dehydrated at a high-altitude, ever!

I never got a chance to spend the night on that pass, outdoors, because father gave the not so experienced junior officers a suggestion on how to clear the pass and by 2:30 at night we had reached our next destination. About 60 miles away.

But not before we finished our chicken dinner, – roasted chicken with lots of butter, and stuffed homemade potato bread with raw onions and lots of lemons and green chilies – food of the gods, especially when one was sooooo hungry – admired the size of the stars and started off again with a loud hail and prayers – everyone does that, on that particular pass, irrespective of caste, creed, or religion.

It is just an invocation to your own God and the power of good to protect you from the wrath of the mountains and bring you back safely home, standing as we were in the lap of ruthless nature, with landslides before us and avalanches behind us.

Let me tell you about one particular piece of equipment, I noticed that was in the pocket of every soldier and officer.

It was a well filled lighter – the ordinary cigarette lighter – None of them were smokers because at that altitude they needed air to breathe had to be hundred percent fit and they really could not afford any other health and breathe destroying stimuli-and after that interesting adventure, I added it to my survival pack.

It was wrapped up in a small packet with some shavings of wood and also some newspaper wrapped around a small magnifying glass, and just a few cotton balls soaked in spirit, in case the stove needed some help in lighting up. Along with that there were a number of large eight hour wax candles in the packet.

I had never heard of fire lighters at that time, but I have heard that they are excellent for lighting campfires and wooden fires. There run about $22 for a packet of 24, a bit too expensive for my pocket!

Until then, I make do with my lighter, light up a candle, and use it for lighting a wood fire.

Of course, lighting a fire is a bit difficult at a high-altitude, where there is a paucity of air and oxygen. Also, if you are outdoors and there is a Gale blowing, the candle in the wind, no pun intended is going to flicker out. So your first job is of course to find shelter.

Never stay out in the open, in harsh weather. This is the easiest way in which you can get sick either due to hypothermia or a lowering of your immunity because you got soaked to the skin.

If it is raining around you, you do not have to bother about water harvesting, because the rain has soaked everything around you and you are going to have lots of water soaking your equipment. After torrential rain, your own first priority is going to be to get rid of all that water, as soon as you can, especially if your equipment is made up of metal.

But if it has not been raining, you are not going to keep those metal items packed. Place them out in the open. In the early morning, there is going to be a thin condensed layer of liquid on the metal, and you can either collect it in a container or just do what I used to do when young, lick it!

Also, any sort of absorbent cloth is going to be placed outside, so that the dew can get absorbed in the cloth. Naturally, you are going to do the collecting of this liquid before sunrise because it takes anywhere between half a minute – in desert areas – to up to four minutes in other areas for the water to evaporate, the moment the sun comes up.

All right, so let us imagine that you are in an area where there are icebergs. Half of the snow is going to be salty, so melting it is a waste of precious fuel. So you need to recognize this particular snow. It is going to be gray in color. It is going to be opaque due to the salt content.

If you are in a situation where there is salty water everywhere and not a drop to drink and the weather is 0° outside, well, you do not need to worry about fresh water.

Collect all that salty water in a large container and put it outside. Allow the surface to freeze, possibly overnight, depending on the temperature. The next morning you are going to have a layer of ice. Break the ice layer and carefully filter off the next layer which is fresh water. Be careful not to disturb the middle layer which is salt and slush. Throw away the slushy salty layer.

Stranded on the Beach

I was just discussing dream holidays with a number of my colleagues about a decade ago and found that many of them preferred not doing any sort of loony adventuring! They liked their creature comforts and when I told them that I did not mind spending a week on a nice little island, with plenty of fruit, vegetables, fish, meat, sun, sand and surf, they went all gleeeep, ants, sand flies, midges, and sand everywhere, getting into everything, and the clinching reason – salt-water.

Believe it or not, if you find yourself stranded on a beach, with salt water everywhere from the sea, and no fresh water source, you do not have to worry at all!

You are just going to go about hundred feet away from the shore. You are going to find some sand dunes, there. Locate the first dune and go behind it. Now dig a hole, to the depth of about 3 – 5 feet.

The bottom is going to be lined with a number of rocks, and also it has a proper supporting wall, so that your hole does not cave in – which is going to be lined with as much wood as you can collect. Come on, you are on a beach, on a tropical island. You have driftwood all around you. You have fronds of coconut and palm. Now sit back and allow the water to seep into your water hole.

Within some hours you are going to have a good collection of water, which is going to include rainwater and also seawater which has been filtered through the sand. If your first sip tastes salty, move away further inside the island, away from the seashore and make a new beach well.

Nobody living next to the sea on a tropical island is ever going to find himself suffering from a paucity of water. He is going to get plenty of rainwater. He is also going to get freshwater especially as it is a tropical atmosphere.

A friend told me this other trick, but it would take a little more time, I would have to make a fire, but I would get water which was salt-less. While the water was seeping in, I would be heating some stones in the fire. When they were really hot, they would be dropped into the water. Immediate steam, caught on a piece of cloth stretched out over the mouth of the hole. Remove the cloth and wring out the water. This was time-consuming, but according to him, this was the way in which the Islanders in the Pacific – Bora-Bora, Maui, Hawaii, Saipan, Okinawa, Easter Island, Tahiti, etc. managed to get salt free water if they were stranded anywhere.

Remember that the rock has to be completely dry before you heat it. If it has any bit of moisture in it, the moment you start applying the heat, the water is going to turn into steam and you are going to have exploding rocks.

Conclusion

This book has given you plenty of interesting tips on how you can find and collect water in order to survive. I am not talking about storage of water in your house, because there are plenty of sites out there talking about storing water in 55 gallon food grade plastic containers, but what use are they going to be, if your property has been totally flattened by Typhoon Tanya or Hurricane Harriet, or earthquake Emeline? And you have no access to all those 55 gallon plastic containers now buried under tons of rubble…

The survival tips given here have been used down the centuries all over the world by people with an instinct to survive. Their first priority and mindset is we are not going to give up. And they do not.

Also, they are sensible enough not to use any substitutes for water because they are too lazy to dig for it or hunt for it. They have those cans of beer, so hey, they have liquid, don't they?!?

Alcohol is the most dangerous substitute, which you can use in place of water. It is debilitating. It is going to wreck your natural state of health. Also, alcohol is capable of clouding your normal sensible state of judgment and you are going to feel a state of euphoria, which is of course going to be temporary. In a alcoholic haze, you are going to believe that nothing can or will happen to you. But you are going to wake up the next morning dehydrated and with a hangover and definitely not in a healthy state of mind, heart, or body.

Do not ever resort to drinking your own body fluids because they are full of toxins, especially urine, which also has about 1.5 – 2% of salt. Here is this system to flush out the poisonous toxins in your body and you are drinking it again, in its unpurified form? Definitely a no-no.

Nevertheless, there are schools of survival where this liquid is purified after condensation – take two bottles, fill one up with this liquid, and use some duct tape to tape the mouth of one bottle to that of another bottle. Place them both in the sun. Condensation from the sun is going to evaporate the liquid from one bottle and it is going to cool and collect in the other bottle.

This was a survival technique taken from an army manual. Not desperate enough to try it or drinking blood which may have an infection already in it along with being really salty. Also, this method is going to allow you to survive for just another couple of days, so you can try this condensed water from urine resort only as the ultimate last resort.

Never ever drink seawater or ice which has been formed from seawater. This is going to dehydrate your body really badly. Instead, dig, dig, dig like the meerkats, but instead of a tunnel, you are going to be digging a hole/well.

Survive, Live Long and Prosper!

Author Bio

Dueep Jyot Singh is a Management and IT Professional who managed to gather Postgraduate qualifications in Management and English and Degrees in Science, French and Education while pursuing different enjoyable career options like being an hospital administrator, IT,SEO and HRD Database Manager/ trainer, movie , radio and TV scriptwriter, theatre artiste and public speaker, lecturer in French, Marketing and Advertising, ex-Editor of Hearts On Fire (now known as Solstice) Books Missouri USA, advice columnist and cartoonist, publisher and Aviation School trainer, ex-moderator on Medico.in, banker, student councilor ,travelogue writer … among other things!

One fine morning, she decided that she had enough of killing herself by Degrees and went back to her first love -- writing. It's more enjoyable! She already has 48 published academic and 14 fiction- in- different- genre books under her belt.

When she is not designing websites or making Graphic design illustrations for clients , she is browsing through old bookshops hunting for treasures, of which she has an enviable collection – including R.L. Stevenson, O.Henry, Dornford Yates, Maurice Walsh, De Maupassant, Victor Hugo, Sapper, C.N. Williamson, "Bartimeus" and the crown of her collection- Dickens "The Old Curiosity Shop," and "Martin Chuzzlewit" and so on… Just call her "Renaissance Woman" - collecting herbal remedies, acting like Universal Helping Hand/Agony Aunt, or escaping to her dear mountains for a bit of exploring, collecting herbs and plants, and trekking.

Check out some of the other JD-Biz Publishing books

Gardening Series on Amazon

Country Life Books

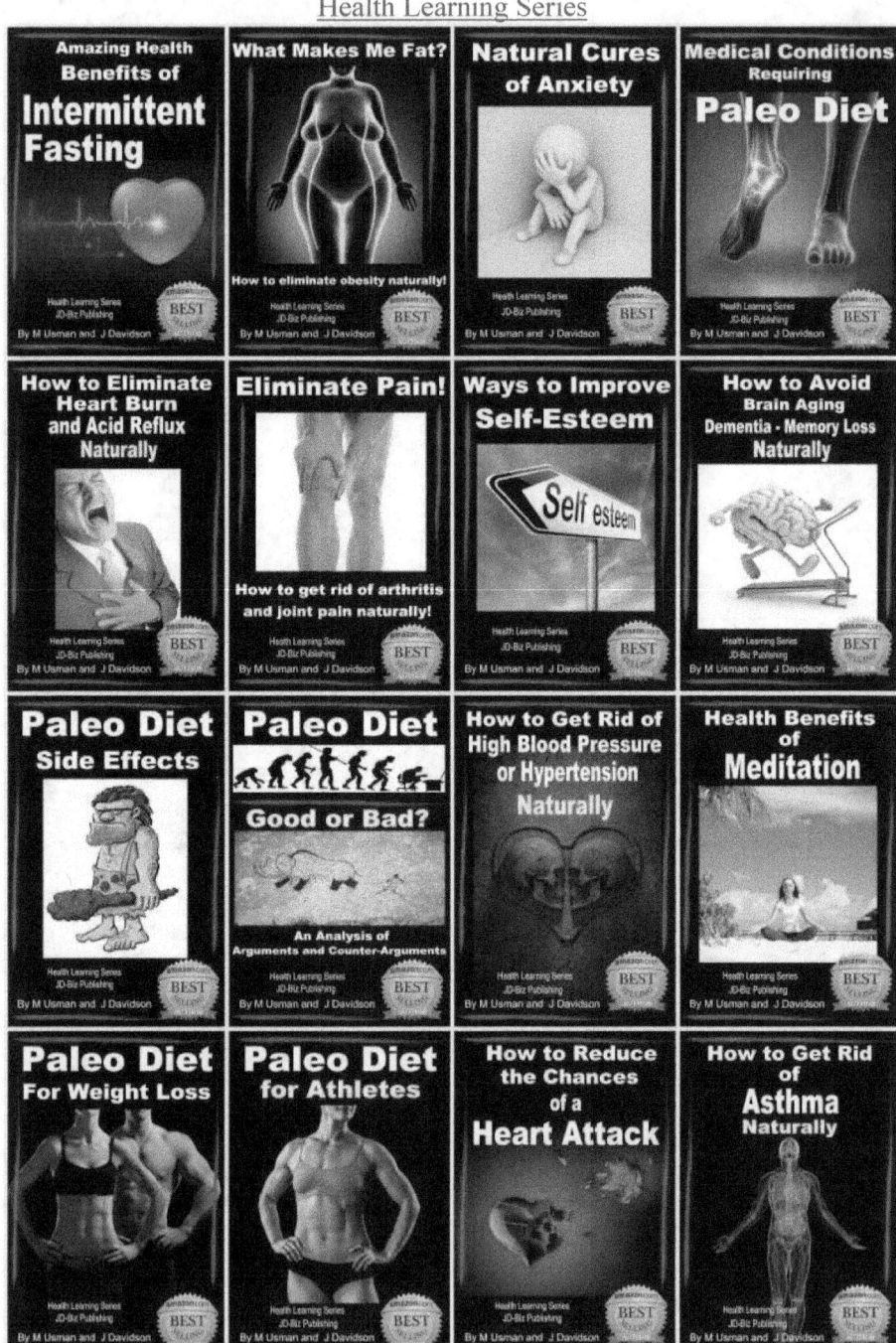

Amazing Animal Book Series

Learn To Draw Series

How to Build and Plan Books

Entrepreneur Book Series

Our books are available at

1. Amazon.com

2. Barnes and Noble

3. Itunes

4. Kobo

5. Smashwords

6. Google Play Books

Download Free Books!

http://MendonCottageBooks.com

Publisher

JD-Biz Corp

P O Box 374

Mendon, Utah 84325

http://www.jd-biz.com/

Mendon Cottage Books
P O Box 374, Mendon Utah 84325